Maximizing Rev[enue] through Social Media: A Guide to Effective Tactics

Introduction

Social media has become an essential tool for businesses looking to reach a wider audience and increase their revenue. With billions of users around the world, social media platforms such as Facebook, Twitter, and Instagram provide companies with a unique opportunity to connect with their target audience and promote their products or services.

However, with so many businesses vying for attention on these platforms, it can be challenging to stand out from the crowd and effectively use social media to drive revenue. This book will provide a comprehensive guide to maximizing revenue through social media, offering practical and effective tactics that can be implemented immediately.

From creating engaging content and leveraging influencer marketing, to analysing metrics and targeting advertisements, this book will cover all the key elements of a successful social media marketing strategy. Whether you're a seasoned marketer or just starting out, this book will give you the knowledge and tools you need to make the most of social media and grow your business.

Index

- Develop a strong social media presence by regularly posting engaging and relevant content.

- Utilise influencer marketing to reach a larger audience and build trust with potential customers.

- Use data and analytics to understand your target audience and tailor your social media strategy accordingly.

- Create and run targeted advertisements to reach specific demographics.

- Engage with your followers and respond promptly to their inquiries and feedback.

- Take advantage of social media features such as live streams and story posts to connect with your audience in real-time.

- Collaborate with other businesses and industry leaders to expand your reach and establish yourself as an authority in your field.

- Offer exclusive promotions and discounts to your social media followers to incentivize them to make a purchase.

- Use eye-catching graphics and visually appealing content to grab the attention of your audience.

- Utilise user-generated content, such as customer reviews and testimonials, to build credibility and trust.

Chapter-1

Develop a strong social media presence by regularly posting engaging and relevant content

Posting regularly and consistently is essential for building a strong social media presence. By doing so, you can keep your followers engaged and interested in your brand. The content you post should be relevant to your target audience and tailored to their interests and needs. Additionally, incorporating visually appealing elements, such as images and videos, can help to grab the attention of your followers and make your content stand out in their feed. When posting, aim to create a balance between promoting your products or services and providing value to your audience through informative or entertaining content.

Developing a strong social media presence is a crucial aspect of any successful marketing strategy. With billions of active users on platforms such as Facebook, Twitter, and Instagram, businesses have a unique opportunity to connect with their target audience and promote their products or services to a large, global audience. To do so effectively, it is essential to post regularly and consistently, in order to keep your followers engaged and interested in your brand.

When creating content for social media, it's important to keep your target audience in mind. The content you post should be relevant to their interests and needs, and tailored to their specific demographic. This could include information about your products or services, industry news, or even entertaining or educational content. In order to stand out from the crowd, it's also important to make your content visually appealing. By incorporating images and videos, you can grab the attention of your followers and make your content more engaging and memorable.

In addition to posting relevant and engaging content, it's also important to be active on social media and respond promptly to any inquiries or feedback from your followers. This helps to build trust and credibility with your audience, and demonstrates your commitment to customer service. Furthermore, by engaging with your followers and encouraging interaction, you can create a sense of community around your brand and foster a deeper connection with your target audience.

Another key aspect of building a strong social media presence is to stay up-to-date with the latest trends and changes on each platform. Social media is constantly evolving, and it's important to be aware of new features and updates in order to make the most of your marketing efforts. For example, platforms such as Instagram and TikTok have recently introduced new features such as Reels and

Live Streams, which provide businesses with new and innovative ways to connect with their audience and promote their products or services.

Finally, it's essential to continuously measure and analyse your social media efforts in order to understand what is working and what is not. This information can be used to identify areas for improvement and make data-driven decisions that will help you to achieve your goals. By utilising analytics tools such as Google Analytics or Facebook Insights, you can track metrics such as engagement, reach, and conversion rates, and use this information to optimise your strategy and drive better results.

In conclusion, building a strong social media presence requires a combination of posting engaging and relevant content, being active and responsive on each platform, staying up-to-date with the latest trends, and continually measuring and analysing your efforts. By implementing these tactics, you can effectively use social media to reach a wider audience, increase your revenue, and establish your brand as a leader in your industry.

Chapter-2

Utilise influencer marketing to reach a larger audience and build trust with potential customers

Influencer marketing is a form of advertising that involves partnering with individuals who have a large following on social media or other online platforms to promote a product or service. It is an effective way of reaching a large audience and building trust with potential customers.

Influencers often have a dedicated and engaged audience who trust their recommendations and opinions, making them a valuable asset to brands looking to reach new customers and establish credibility. When an influencer endorses a product or service, it can help to generate buzz and drive sales.

To get started with influencer marketing, brands should identify influencers who align with their values and target audience. This will help to ensure that the content produced by the influencer is authentic and resonates with their followers. Brands can then negotiate a partnership agreement with the influencer, outlining the goals and expectations for the campaign.

It's important to remember that influencer marketing is a two-way street. Brands should be willing to invest in the partnership and provide the influencer with the resources and support they need to create high-quality content. This can include providing them with product samples, offering compensation for their time and effort, or providing access to exclusive events and experiences.

When it comes to measuring the success of an influencer marketing campaign, it's important to track both the reach and engagement of the content produced by the influencer. This can be done by monitoring metrics such as likes, comments, and shares, as well as tracking conversions and sales.

It's also worth noting that influencer marketing is not a one-size-fits-all approach and may not be right for every brand. Brands should consider their target audience and marketing goals, as well as their budget, before deciding whether to invest in influencer marketing.

In conclusion, influencer marketing is a powerful tool that can help brands to reach a larger audience and build trust with potential customers. By partnering with the right influencer and providing them with the resources and support they need to succeed, brands can create engaging and impactful content that resonates with their target audience.

Chapter-3

Use data and analytics to understand your target audience and tailor your social media strategy accordingly

Data and analytics play a crucial role in understanding the target audience for any social media strategy. By gathering information about the preferences, behaviours and interests of the target audience, businesses can tailor their social media presence to reach and engage with the right people.

Here's a summary of how data and analytics can be used to understand and tailor social media strategy:

1. Demographic data: This information helps to understand the age, gender, location and education level of the target audience. This data can be obtained through social media analytics tools or surveys.

2. Interests and behaviours: By tracking the content that people are engaging with, businesses can gain insights into the topics and interests that matter most to their target audience. This information can be used to create content that resonates with the audience and encourages them to engage with the brand.

3. Social media platform preferences: Different platforms have different audiences, and it's important to understand which ones are most popular among the target audience. For example, if the target audience is largely Gen Z, then TikTok may be a platform to consider, whereas if the target audience is Baby Boomers, then Facebook may be the better choice.

4. Customer engagement: Measuring the engagement rate on social media can help businesses understand how well their content is resonating with the target audience. If the engagement rate is low, then the content or messaging may need to be adjusted.

5. Sentiment analysis: This involves analysing the tone of conversations on social media to

determine if they are positive, negative, or neutral. This information can be used to identify areas of improvement in the brand's social media presence.

Once the data has been collected and analysed, businesses can use the insights to develop a tailored social media strategy. For example, if the target audience is interested in eco-friendly products, then the brand can focus on creating content around sustainability and environmental issues. Additionally, if the target audience is largely on Instagram, then the brand may want to invest in visually appealing content and influencer marketing.

In conclusion, data and analytics are critical components of a successful social media strategy. By understanding the target audience, businesses can create content that resonates with the right people and drives engagement on social media.

Chapter-4

Create and run targeted advertisements to reach specific demographics

Targeted advertising is a marketing technique that allows businesses to reach specific demographics with their advertisements. This is done by analysing consumer data, such as age, location, interests, and online behaviour, and using this information to create advertisements that are tailored to their needs and preferences.

To create targeted advertisements, the first step is to identify your target demographic. This involves looking at your existing customer data and analysing their characteristics, such as age, location, income, and interests. You can also gather this information from consumer surveys, social media, and market research reports.

Once you have a clear understanding of your target demographic, you can start creating advertisements that are tailored to their needs and preferences. This involves using images, language, and messaging that resonate with your target audience. For example, if your target demographic is young adults, you might use bright colours, bold graphics, and a casual tone in your advertisements.

To run targeted advertisements, you will need to choose a platform that allows you to reach your target demographic. This could be a social media platform, such as Facebook or Instagram, or a search engine, such as Google AdWords. Each platform has its own set of targeting options, so it is important to understand the options available and choose the one that best suits your needs.

Once you have chosen a platform, you will need to set up your advertisement. This involves creating a campaign, setting your budget, and selecting the targeting options that best suit your needs. For example, if you want to target a specific location, you might select the option to target people in that area. If you want to target people who are interested in a specific topic, you might select the option to target people who have engaged with similar content in the past.

Finally, it is important to regularly monitor and adjust your targeted advertisements to ensure that they are reaching your target demographic and achieving the desired results. This might involve changing the images, language, or messaging in your advertisements, or adjusting your targeting options.

In conclusion, targeted advertising is a powerful marketing tool that allows businesses to reach specific demographics with their advertisements. By understanding your target demographic, creating advertisements that resonate with their needs and preferences, and using the right platform to reach them, businesses can achieve greater success with their marketing efforts.

Chapter-5

Engage with your followers and respond promptly to their inquiries and feedback

Engaging with followers and responding promptly to their inquiries and feedback is an important part of social media management. This is because it helps to build a relationship with your audience, establish trust, and provide a positive experience for your followers.

To engage with your followers, you can use a variety of methods, such as responding to comments on posts, liking and sharing content from followers, and running social media contests and polls. You can also take advantage of direct messaging features to respond to inquiries and provide support.

It's important to respond promptly to feedback, as this shows that you value your followers and are committed to providing a positive experience for them. Responding in a timely manner also helps to resolve issues quickly and effectively, which can improve customer satisfaction and prevent negative reviews from spreading on social media.

When responding to inquiries and feedback, it's important to use a friendly and professional tone. Avoid using language that is defensive or dismissive, and take the time to listen to your followers and understand their concerns. You should also be transparent about your intentions and actions, and keep your followers informed about any updates or changes.

In addition to engaging with followers and responding to their inquiries and feedback, it's important to regularly monitor your social media presence to identify any potential issues or areas for improvement. This can involve using social media management tools to track engagement, monitor brand mentions, and analyse your audience's behaviour.

Overall, engaging with your followers and responding promptly to their inquiries and feedback is an essential part of social media management.

By building relationships with your audience, providing a positive experience, and regularly monitoring your social media presence, you can improve customer satisfaction and grow your online community.

Chapter-6

Take advantage of social media features such as live streams and story posts to connect with your audience in real-time

Social media platforms offer a variety of features for businesses to connect with their audience in real-time. Live streams and story posts are two such features that can be leveraged to build a strong online presence and engage with your target audience.

Live streams allow businesses to broadcast real-time video content to their followers. This type of content is highly engaging, as it offers a sense of exclusivity and immediacy to the audience. Live streams can be used to host Q&A sessions, product demonstrations, behind-the-scenes tours, and more. They provide an opportunity for businesses to build trust and establish a personal connection with their audience.

Story posts, available on platforms such as Instagram and Snapchat, are short-lived content pieces that disappear after 24 hours. They offer businesses the opportunity to share quick, candid updates with their followers, such as product launches, sneak peeks, and exclusive promotions. This type of content is particularly effective in building anticipation and excitement around upcoming events and products.

To make the most of these features, businesses should plan their content in advance and promote their live streams and story posts to their audience. Additionally, they should interact with their audience during the live stream or story post and respond to their questions and comments in real-time. This type of engagement will help to build a loyal community of followers and improve the overall impact of your social media efforts.

In conclusion, live streams and story posts are valuable tools for businesses looking to connect with their audience in real-time. By leveraging these features, businesses can build trust and establish a personal connection with their followers, ultimately driving greater engagement and building a stronger online presence.

Chapter-7

Collaborate with other businesses and industry leaders to expand your reach and establish yourself as an authority in your field

Collaborating with other businesses and industry leaders is a great way to expand your reach and establish yourself as an authority in your field. By partnering with other companies and leaders, you can gain access to their networks, resources, and expertise, helping you to grow your business and reach new audiences. This kind of collaboration can also help to build credibility and demonstrate your commitment to your industry, positioning you as a thought leader and trusted expert.

To begin, you should research potential collaborators and identify companies and leaders who share your values and goals. You may want to consider partnering with businesses that complement your offerings, or those who serve similar target markets. You could also reach out to industry associations or attend conferences and networking events to connect with other professionals and build relationships.

Once you have identified potential collaborators, it is important to approach the relationship in a strategic and professional manner. Consider what each party can bring to the table, and develop a clear plan for how the collaboration will work. Be open and transparent about your goals and expectations, and ensure that all parties are aligned on the key objectives.

It is also important to establish clear lines of communication and regularly check in with your collaborators to ensure that the relationship is working effectively. You may want to establish regular meetings or conference calls, or set up an online platform where you can share updates and resources.

By working together, you can pool your resources and expertise, and benefit from each other's strengths. This could involve co-hosting events, co-creating content, or jointly promoting each other's products or services. By leveraging each other's networks and reputation, you can expand your reach and raise your profile, positioning yourself as a leader in your field.

In conclusion, collaborating with other businesses and industry leaders can be a valuable way to grow your business and establish yourself as an authority in your field. To be successful, it is important to approach these relationships in a strategic and professional manner, and to communicate effectively to ensure that everyone is aligned and working towards the same goals.

Chapter-8

Offer exclusive promotions and discounts to your social media followers to incentivize them to make a purchase

Offering exclusive promotions and discounts to social media followers can be a great way to incentivize them to make a purchase. To get started, you'll need to build a strong social media presence and engage with your followers regularly. Once you have a solid following, you can begin to offer them special deals and promotions that are not available to the general public.

One way to do this is to create unique discount codes for your followers, which they can use to receive a certain percentage off their purchases. This can be promoted through social media posts, direct messages, or even email newsletters. The key is to make these promotions feel exclusive and special, so your followers feel valued and motivated to make a purchase.

Another way to incentivize your followers is to offer limited-time promotions, such as flash sales or 24-hour deals. This creates a sense of urgency and encourages followers to act quickly and take advantage of the offer. You can also consider offering special bonuses, such as free shipping or a complimentary gift with purchase, to sweeten the deal.

It's important to measure the success of your promotions and adjust your strategy accordingly. Track the number of followers who make a purchase using the promotion and the amount of revenue generated. Use this information to refine your approach and determine what works best for your audience.

In addition to incentivizing followers to make a purchase, these promotions can also help to build brand loyalty. By making your followers feel valued and offering them unique perks, you are creating a strong emotional connection with them. This can help to drive repeat business and increase overall customer satisfaction.

In conclusion, offering exclusive promotions and discounts to your social media followers can be a powerful way to incentivize them to make a purchase. By creating a sense of exclusivity, urgency, and value, you can increase your conversion rate and build brand loyalty. With the right strategy and execution, this approach can be a win-win for both your business and your followers.

Chapter-9

Use eye-catching graphics and visually appealing content to grab the attention of your audience

Using eye-catching graphics and visually appealing content is an effective way to grab the attention of your audience. It is important to note that the visuals should not only be attractive, but also relevant to the message you are trying to convey. Visuals can include images, graphs, charts, infographics, and other graphic elements. The use of these elements can make your content more engaging and help your audience retain information more effectively.

Incorporating eye-catching graphics can help break up the monotony of long blocks of text and make your content more visually appealing. Bright colours, interesting patterns, and creative layouts can all help capture the attention of your audience. You can use graphics to highlight key points, illustrate complex information, or simply add a touch of visual interest to your content.

Another way to make your content visually appealing is to use high-quality images. The images you use should be relevant to your message and of a high resolution. Avoid using stock images that are overused or unoriginal, as this can detract from the overall impact of your content.

In addition to eye-catching graphics, it is also important to consider the overall layout and design of your content. A well-designed layout can make your content easier to read and navigate, and can help guide your audience's attention to the most important parts of your message.

In conclusion, using eye-catching graphics and visually appealing content is an effective way to grab the attention of your audience. By incorporating high-quality visuals and a well-designed layout, you can make your content more engaging and memorable, and increase the chances that your message will be retained and acted upon.

Chapter-10

Utilise user-generated content, such as customer reviews and testimonials, to build credibility and trust

User-generated content, also known as UGC, is a type of content created by customers or users of a product or service. This type of content can come in various forms, such as reviews, testimonials, ratings, comments, images, videos, and more. Utilising UGC is a powerful way to build credibility and trust with potential customers.

One of the main benefits of UGC is that it is created by customers who have actually used the product or service, and therefore, their opinions and experiences are more trustworthy and relatable to other potential customers. UGC is also seen as more honest and authentic than traditional marketing content, which can often be perceived as biassed or overly promotional.

Incorporating UGC into a company's marketing strategy can also help to increase engagement with potential customers. UGC can create a sense of community and interaction, as customers feel like they are able to contribute their own thoughts and experiences. This can lead to higher levels of customer loyalty and advocacy for the brand.

Another advantage of UGC is that it can help to improve search engine optimization (SEO). Google and other search engines consider user-generated content to be a trustworthy and relevant source of information, and therefore, websites that feature UGC may be more likely to appear at the top of search engine results pages.

It is also important to note that UGC can provide valuable insights into customer opinions and preferences, allowing companies to make informed decisions about their products and services. By regularly monitoring and analysing UGC, companies can gain a better understanding of what customers like and dislike, and make improvements accordingly.

In conclusion, incorporating user-generated content into a company's marketing strategy is a powerful way to build credibility and trust with potential customers. UGC can provide valuable insights, increase engagement and loyalty, and improve search engine optimization. Companies should consider using UGC in their marketing efforts to enhance the customer experience and drive business success.

www.ingramcontent.com/pod-product-compliance
Lightning Source LLC
LaVergne TN
LVHW072053060326
832903LV00054B/419